The Way of
Leading People

Sensei:

With appreciation for all you've
done to bring Aikido to the
world ~ this book could
never have been without you

:)

Tim

The Way of Leading People

Unlocking Your
Integral Leadership Skills
with the *Tao Te Ching*

Patrick J. Warneka
Timothy H. Warneka
Lao Tzu

Asogomi Publishing International
Cleveland, Ohio

First printing 2007.

Cover & Interior Design by: Asogomi Publishing International
Editor: Cheri Laser

LCCN: 2006907769
ISBN: 978-0-9768627-4-1

Published by:
Asogomi Publishing International,
P.O. Box 20, Cleveland, Ohio 44092

SPECIAL SALES:
Asogomi Publishing International books are available at special bulk purchase discounts to use for sales promotion, premiums, gifts, increasing magazine subscriptions or renewals, and educational purposes. Special books or book excerpts can also be created to fit your organization's specific needs. For information, please contact Asogomi Publishing International, P.O. Box 20, Cleveland, OH 44092, or email: Sales@asogomi.com.

This book is dedicated to every leader who understands that serving both people and the bottom line are not mutually exclusive goals.

Foreword

Somewhere in the late 1960's, I was handed a dog-eared copy of the *Tao Te Ching* by a philosophy professor who added the dubious comment, "This is something you'd probably like." The small paperback was held in place by rubber bands, and the yellowed pages kept falling out. The actual text of the book occupied a small space next to the dense, endless commentary by a nineteenth century English scholar who was the editor and translator. There were no glossy photos, hand-brushed calligraphy, or slick vellum pages. This was clearly not intended to be an elegant, coffee table book.

Yet thumbing through the crumbling pages, I was immediately captivated. The book was mysterious, puzzling, and maddeningly paradoxical—impenetrable and at the same time compelling. The words made sense to my heart and gut, but not to my head. Who was this Lao Tzu, and what was he really saying? I returned over and over again to the economical lines, not because I learned something but because, in some inexplicable way, reading the book made me feel more settled.

A year or so later I began a meditation practice, and a year or so after that I began practicing Aikido, a Japanese martial art. As these practices began to inform my life, they ran on a parallel course with my relationship with the Tao. Stepping on a path of meditation and Aikido—living the *Tao,* in other words—has allowed the depth and profundity of the *Tao Te Ching* to permeate my whole being more readily.

Of all the editions of the *Tao Te Ching* that I've carried over these years, Patrick and Tim Warneka's *The Way of Leading People* is by far the most innovative and daring. The stunning photographs of urban cityscapes instead of nature aren't the only things that make the book unique. There's also the emphasis on a compassionate, post-rational leadership that builds a dynamic relevancy for the sustainability of the planet and the human race.

In these interpretations of the verses, you'll find stimulating and applicable references to the *Internet, body-mind continuum, emotional engagement, CEO's, copy machines, mission statements,* and much, much more. This book will provoke the reader's thinking around leading others and walking your personal path, as we all discover how to lead a life of harmony in a technologically heavy, post-rational world.

The Warnekas challenge us to open our hearts and minds and let the 2500-year-old wisdom of this classic text interface directly with our 21st century concerns. I suggest you choose a verse to read everyday and allow the wisdom of the words and the impact of the photographs to work through your spirit. Then step on a path, a living discipline, and let yourself embody your personal *Tao.*

Richard Strozzi-Heckler, Ph.D.
Author of *The Leadership Dojo, The Anatomy of Change* and *In Search of the Warrior Spirit*
Strozzi Institute,
Petaluma, California
3 September 2006

Post-Rational Leadership, Lao Tzu, and the *Tao Te Ching*

Lao Tzu, or Master Lao as we in the West would call him, was a Chinese sage who lived around 600 B.C. and whose life story has faded into semi-mythical status. As legend recounts, Master Lao, renowned for his wisdom, repeatedly refused to write any of his insights down, mistrusting the confinement of the written word. Toward the end of his life, saddened by people's unwillingness to live in accordance with natural law, Master Lao decided to retreat into the wilderness. Heading toward what is now Tibet, Master Lao passed through one of the many gates in the Great Wall of China. A gatekeeper, Yin Xi by name, persuaded old Lao Tzu to record his teachings. The result was the 5000-character *Tao Te Ching* (pronounced *Dow Duh Jing*)—one of the most important texts in human history. This book, the title of which translates roughly as "The Book of How Life Works," is an instruction manual for living in accord with what Chinese philosophy calls *Tao*, the ultimate ground of being—the Eternal.

In his wisdom, Master Lao understood something 2500 years ago that we in the West are only now just beginning to appreciate: *that rational thinking is not the final stage of human development.* While the Western world has long held rational thought to be the epitome of human development, new research is in agreement with Master Lao, pointing to other ways of thinking beyond (read: *better than*) rationality. Scientists are eagerly investigating these newly identified "post-rational" ways of knowledge, describing them by many names: contemporary philosopher Ken Wilber speaks of *vision-logic;* Malcolm Gladwell refers to "the power of thinking without thinking" with the *adaptive unconscious;* in the Emotional Intelligence literature the movement is categorized under several names. Indeed, this post-rational stage of knowing have been under observation for some years: Swiss psychiatrist C. G. Jung and his Jungian followers call it *intuition;* the great martial artist Bruce Lee referred to this higher stage of awareness as "It"; and Zen masters throughout the ages simply use the term *mushin* (literally, *no mind*, as in, "beyond rational thought"). For interested readers, current research into post-rational ways of knowing can be found in Malcolm Gladwell's best-selling *Blink*; Gary Klein's *The Power of Intuition;* Ken Wilber's *Sex, Ecology & Spirituality;* and Goleman, Boyatzis & McKee's *Primal Leadership*, among others. For an actual experience of post-rational development, practice Aikido, or Yoga, or T'ai Chi, or meditation, or a similar bodymind practice for five to ten years ... or more.

Post-rational awareness is beyond words: paradoxical, mysterious and powerful. If post-rationality could be easily conveyed in words, there would be no need for the strict meditative practices of Zen, for the sweat and exertion of Aikido or Yoga or countless other body-centered practices. Written over 2500 years ago, the *Tao Te Ching* is one of the earliest recorded attempts to describe this post-rational way of living in harmony with the world. Wisely, Master Lao understood that, where prose fails, poetry succeeds. While prose is unable to fully capture these post-rational developmental levels, poetry's strength emerges by not even trying. By allowing space for metaphors to expand, poetry taps into the wisdom of post-rationality in ways that allow our rational minds to glimpse that higher level of knowing. Since Master Lao wrote most of the *Tao Te Ching* in poetry, the present authors have tried to stay true to his legacy.

Today, more than ever, leaders need the wisdom of Lao Tzu. Master Lao recognized the importance of *personal transformation* for leaders. Simply reading new material or being exposed to new ideas is not enough for today's leaders. In order to be successful in today's global economy, leaders must have the courage to *change*—to step forward into the post-rational realm, thereby becoming better leaders ... and better people. The human race is at a crucial crossroads, and nothing else will suffice in today's world.

Welcome to *The Way of Leading People: Unlocking Your Integral Leadership Skills with the Tao Te Ching.*

NOTE TO THE READER

The written number on each page references the relevant verse number from the *Tao Te Ching*. The numbers are not page numbers. As this book features selected interpretations from the *Tao Te Ching*, the verse numbers are not always consecutive.

What you are about to read is a modern interpretation of Lao Tzu's *Tao Te Ching*. The authors have respectfully updated Master Lao's words in order to apply the spirit of these words to the global realities that face us in the 21st century.

TIM'S THOUGHTS

When most people think of the *Tao Te Ching*, they think of nature—of trees and rocks, streams and mountains. This is fitting, because the early Chinese Taoists saw the Eternal (which they called the *Tao*) reflected in nature and often retreated into the forests and mountains to seek that connection. What many people do not know is that these same Taoists were also quite interested in practical technology. Their appreciation of the natural world made them the world's first scientists, searching for ways to bridge nature and technology (for more, see Robert Temple's brilliant book *The Genius of China*). When I first saw Patrick's pictures, I was struck by how powerfully they, too, bridged nature and technology. On film, Patrick so strongly captures the essence of the *Tao* in an urban setting—the naturalness of technology in the stone, steel, and structure of city architecture—that I knew we had to share them. Thus, *The Way of Leading People* was born.

Those ancient Taoists would have loved Patrick's pictures. His photographs teach us that we do not need to escape to the forests and mountains to discover the Eternal. Viewing these images, we learn that *Tao* is right here, right now, amidst the concrete and traffic lights, the cubicles and paperwork that comprise life in the great cities throughout the world. I have my favorite pictures for remembering these lessons—and I am certain you will find yours.

Besides Patrick's pictures, my interpretation of this classic text draws inspiration from a number of sources, including (in no particular order): Miyamoto Musashi's *A Book of Five Rings*; mythologist Joseph Campbell; Jane English's & Gia-Fu Feng's *Tao Te Ching*; Ken Wilber; Carl Jung; Malcolm Gladwell; Sun Tzu's *Art of War;* the writings and art of Master Morihei Ueshiba, the founder of Aikido—especially as that discipline has been passed on to me by my sensei Akira Tohei, Paul Linden and Mary Heiny; my book *Leading People the Black Belt Way*; Gestalt Psychology; current research on Emotional Intelligence; and writings from various world wisdom traditions. Following the Taoist practice of valuing simplicity, I attempted to distill these words to the fewest possible, knowing that the space *between* the words is what really matters. Being an academic at heart, I was tempted to add footnotes and commentary in order to explain some of the references. Instead, I will hold my peace, letting the words and pictures act as a Rorschach of sorts, allowing you to fill in the "space between" from your own experience. Enjoy the book.

PATRICK'S THOUGHTS

For years now, Tim and I have had a running conversation about leadership. When he first showed me the *Tao Te Ching* I recognized the universal qualities of the leadership principals we had been exploring in our conversations. In these rapidly changing times, leaders today need to be reminded of the fundamentals of leadership, that indeed leadership basics are more important than the latest, greatest idea to come along. In the martial arts, a fighter who has mastered the basics will always defeat a fighter with flashy and intricate techniques. The same is true of leadership. As a leader, when you master the basics of leadership—the essence of which is outlined in this book— you will prevail over leaders who constantly change their approach to fit the leadership fad *du jour*.

Growth, strength, motion, harmony, and *success.* In words and pictures, these fundamental leadership concepts are on display for all to see throughout this book. I invite you to allow the words and pictures within to continue coaching you about the timeless fundamentals of leadership. I enjoyed making this book with my only brother. I hope you learn from the pages within.

ONE

The Way of Leading People that can be fully explained
is never True Leadership.
An element of mystery must remain.
Ways of Leading People that can be completely understood
are not the eternal Ways.
True Leadership begins with words
and ends in the Wordless.
The doorway to eternal mystery.

TWO

Leaders exist only when at least one follows.
"Leader" and "follower" therefore complete each other.
They are two sides of the same coin.
The true leader does nothing,
Yet everything gets done.

THREE

Everyone plays a part in the whole,
Putting one before another leads to strife.
Great leaders transform themselves,
Supporting the same in others.
"Move in harmony with the cosmos propelled by the Divine."
Motion is crucial to the Way of Leading People.

FOUR

Great leadership begins with the body.
Balancing the many with the few.
Breathing.
Connecting with All.

SIX

Great leaders understand:
Give up Strength to get to the Power.
Never forcing,
Yin always wins.

SEVEN

"Leader" and "follower" last forever.
You are but one in a line of many.
To wisely lead people requires following.
Detaching from each, be connected to All.

EIGHT

A wise leader emulates water.
She gains strength from the low.
In leading, flow.
In speech, clarity.
In decisions, just.
In action, presence.

No pushing, no pulling:
No blame.

NINE

Better to stop sooner than to over-reach and stumble.
Claiming undue credit weakens the team.
Failing to listen creates strife.
Stand together when the work is complete:
The path of success.

TEN

Consider body, mind & emotion as one.
How can they be separated?
Listening openly to all things,
Is there nothing you cannot do?
Sparking engagement without dominating,
Feeling emotion without losing control,
Placing credit where it belongs,
This is the Way of Leading People.

ELEVEN

A hotel lobby functions well
Because of the space within.
The Internet has power
Because it connects everyone.

Therefore the wise leader values
space and connection
with people.

TWELVE

Feelings are the foundation of thought.
Emotions give color and texture to every idea.
In the blink of an eye, a decision is made,
A tipping point reached.

Therefore the wise leader is guided by
both his feelings and thoughts.

THIRTEEN

Accept honest mistakes willingly.
Realize error as the human condition.

What do you mean by "Accept honest mistakes willingly"?
Honest mistakes occur.
Do not be concerned.
This is called "accepting honest mistakes willingly."

What do you mean by "Realize error as the human condition"?
Do you know anyone who has not erred?
Leading people with humility creates success.

FOURTEEN

Move with the present.
Lead people in the moment.
When leaders neither push nor pull
Willingly, the people follow.
See, it cannot be measured—leadership beyond form.
Look, it cannot be reasoned—leadership beyond thought.
Understanding leadership beyond thought is the Way of Leading People.

FIFTEEN

Leaders of tomorrow—if they are to be at all—
will be subtle, embodied, and responsive.
Their leadership knowledge beyond measure.
Because measuring their leadership is not possible,
All we can do
Is describe their behavior.
Connected in relationship to all things
Yet standing alone.
Exploring the depths of the outer
While plumbing the space of the inner.
Until outer and inner become One.
Far beyond flatland.

SIXTEEN

The frontiers of leadership
Are within you.

A true leader is empty
And watches the watcher.

When leaders lead people
With just enough words,
Then people look around with pride
Saying, "Look what we did!"

EIGHTEEN

When embodied leadership is forgotten,
Many rules arise.
When emotional engagement leaves a company,
Slogans and mottos emerge.
When an organization is confused,
Vision statements appear.

NINETEEN

Give up knowing, renounce "we-do-it-this-way,"
Everyone succeeds.

Give up slogans, renounce "zero defects,"
Profits soar.

Give up form, renounce emptiness:
Are they not the same?

How much more important
To simply lead,
To deeply connect,
To focus on "we"?

TWENTY-TWO

Discover yin and be victorious;
Success comes from yielding at the right moment.
Embrace "we" and succeed;
Together move forward.
Seek strength in unity and prevail.
Grab for power alone—poverty.

TWENTY-THREE

A wise leader speaks less than she listens.
What good is an open-door policy
With a closed-minded leader?

A thunder clap does not last an hour;
A snowstorm does not last a month.
Why is this?

This is the way of Heaven and Earth.
If Heaven and Earth cannot make things last forever,
Should leaders try and do otherwise?

TWENTY-FOUR

She who is pushed resists.
He who gets pulled pulls back.
A wise leader neither pushes nor pulls.
Instead he blends with "What is."
Pushing and pulling others creates success in the short run;
Significant damage over time.

TWENTY-FIVE

The Way is great;
The Kosmos is great;
Planet Earth is great;
The leader is also great.
These are the four great powers of existence.

Leaders must follow Earth,
for Earth follows the Kosmos,
which follows the Way.

The Way follows nothing but itself.

TWENTY-SIX

Small sits at the base of the Great;
Stillness overcomes Chaos.
The leader, working all day,
Does not forget his humanity.
Though beautiful rewards surround him,
He remains detached and at peace.

To be Great, one recalls the Small.
Given over to Chaos, one abandons Stillness.

TWENTY-SEVEN

Yielding to flow,
A wise leader attends to all things,
Leaving nothing undone.

What is a wise leader?
A teacher of those who follow her.
What of *them*?
They follow the wise leader's lead.
Leader. Follower.
Neither can exist without the other.
Forget this, chaos ensues—a paradoxical mystery.

TWENTY-NINE

Do you think you understand the problem?
Not likely.
Your organization is like an orchestra,
Changing one part creates dissonance,
Like scratchings on a chalk board.
For success, the entire group must play together.
Therefore, the wise leader changes the song, not the parts.

THIRTY

When leaders use power carelessly,
Resistance arises.
Profits decline when power is abused.
The wise leader does what is called for,
Only that.
Never taking advantage of power.

THIRTY-ONE

Pushing and pulling are weapons of fear; all employees hate them.
Therefore the wise leader does not use them.
The successful leader prefers the straight,
While the poor leader twists.

Manipulation is an instrument of fear; not a wise leader's tool.
He never uses it.
While success is dear to his heart,
Victory over others never leads to celebration.

The wise leader finds no merit in victory over others,
knowing that victory over *self* is what counts most.

THIRTY-TWO

"Leading People" remains forever undefined.
With multiple meanings, this discipline cannot be contained in words.
If presidents and CEO's could harness this insight.
They could create ten thousand successful companies.
"Chop wood, carry water, keep practicing."
These are all One to the True Leader.

When the One is divided, new paradigms arise.

Leaders must know when to stop.
Knowing when to stop creates success,
While "Leading People" remains undefined.

THIRTY-THREE

Know your employees: wisdom.
Know yourself: enlightenment.
Directing others requires force.
Directing yourself, discipline.

The leader who respects his team is wealthy.
Staying the course—a sign of discipline.
True leaders contain the space.

THIRTY-FOUR

True leadership flows in all directions.
All departments require this flow.
Which quietly moves toward success;
"Just doing my job."

True leadership supports every department,
Yet seeks no praise.
Aimless, it never misses.

Those who lead people do not seek greatness,
And, therefore, they are truly great.

THIRTY-SIX

To know success,
Leaders must experience failure.
For true success,
Leaders must pay their dues.

Nothing important happens overnight.
This is simply the way of things.

This, then, is the foundation of leading people:
Everything begins—
Everything ends.

THIRTY-SEVEN

Great leaders practice non-action,
Yet everything is completed.
What do you mean by "practicing non-action"?
Not using force. Trusting people to do what they were hired to do.
This is called "practicing non-action."
If managers and supervisors understood this,
All departments would rise to their strengths.
In this way: Success!

THIRTY-EIGHT

A truly great leader is not aware of her greatness,
And therefore is great.
A poor leader tries to be great,
And therefore is not great.

A truly great leader does nothing,
Yet everything gets finished.
A poor leader tries to do everything,
And nothing gets done.

When a poor leader pushes people,
People push her back.
When a poor leader pulls,
People pull against her.

When a poor leader meets with resistance,
She forces things.
Everything stops.

A truly great leader simply leads people.
And everything gets done.

FORTY

The great leader moves in spirals,
Yielding is his strength.
All success comes from great leadership.
Great leadership comes from not leading.

FORTY-ONE

The best leader learns of "leading people"
and strives to do so.
The mediocre leader learns of "leading people"
and tries it once or twice.
The foolish leader learns of "leading people"
and rejects it as nonsense.
If there was no rejection by the foolish,
"leading people" would not be true.

FORTY-TWO

Great leadership starts with one.
From one, two.
From two, three.
From three, an entire organization.

When people within create harmony,
The organization succeeds.

Leaders add through subtraction,
And subtract through addition.

What many have taught, I also teach:
"In the end, violent leaders *always* fail!"
This is the essence of my teaching.

FORTY-THREE

The softest leader
Always triumphs over the hardest leader.

Learn the value of non-action.

Leading people without pushing or pulling
Is understood by too few.

FORTY-FOUR

Up or Down: Which is best?
Push or Pull: Which is worse?
Lead or Follow: Which is more important?

Leaders who care will be unsuccessful.
"Can you care enough not to care?"
An unattached leader gains the most.
She understands the meaning of "not to care,"
And the bottom line grows.

FORTY-SIX

When great leadership is present,
The copy machines hum.
When an organization lacks great leaders,
The organization seeks to "crush the competition."

Do you remember your mission statement?
A lonely paper on the wall
Neither creates engagement nor builds the bottom line,
Even in the finest of frames.

Without leaving your organization, know the planet.
Without leaving your office, understand the universe.
More go, less know.

The wise leader knows without speaking.
He sees without seeing.
He leads without doing.

A true leader is the servant of others.
Understand this and succeed.

FORTY-EIGHT

For becoming a "better leader": an action-plan every day.
For "leading people": no action-plans.

In true leadership,
Less is more.
When great leaders do nothing, nothing is left undone.

The organization succeeds by allowing things to progress,
And fails when leaders interfere.

FORTY-NINE

The greatest leader forgets herself
And attends to the development of others.

Good leaders support excellent workers.
Great leaders support the bottom ten percent.

Great leaders know that
The diamond in the rough
Is always found "in the rough."

FIFTY

In every organization,
Twenty percent emotionally connect,
While eighty percent do not,
Thereby losing revenues.

Why is this so?
The leaders have failed.

Great leaders seek
To engage the eighty percent.

FIFTY-ONE

Can you lead people without support?
Your parents fed you
And paid for college.
Your mentors helped you
Climb the ranks.
You breathe the air,
Eat the food,
Drink the water.

Why should you expect *others* to succeed without support?

FIFTY-TWO

The beginning of a project
Is the most crucial time.
The great oak
Grows from the small acorn.

Great leaders gain power
By yielding their power at the start.

FIFTY-THREE

Is the president of an organization truly worth
Four hundred times the salary of a worker?

When McMansions are built,
The homeless walk the street.
Enormous cars drive by
grandmothers walking barefoot in the snow.
Some children are in private schools,
While others play on broken glass.
"I have mine."

How much is enough?
This is certainly not the Way of Leading People.

FIFTY-FOUR

Listen!
The people are unhappy.
Look!
The organization is losing money.

Listen to employees as employees;
Listen to teams as teams;
Look at departments as departments;
Look at the organization as an organization.

How do I know the organization is losing money?
By looking! By listening!
Eighty-percent will tell me why.

FIFTY-FIVE

Wise leaders do not rush about
Shouting and screaming.
Wasted energy depletes the organization;
Failure is sure to follow.
This is not the Way of Leading People.
What is contrary to the Way does not succeed.

FIFTY-SIX

Leaders who know do not boast.
Leaders who boast do not know.

The wise leader guards his words,
Simplifies his directives.
Leaving people to their work,
He supports and informs.

The wisest leader
Is unconcerned with outcome.
"Trust the process,"
Everything resolves.

FIFTY-SEVEN

Lead an organization justly;
Launch products boldly.
Success comes without striving.
This is the Way of Leading People.

Too many rules,
People cannot breathe.
Too many directives
Create strife.
The more regulations and rules,
The more people cheat.

Therefore, the wise leader says,
    "I decrease rules and people prosper.
     I let people work and the organization grows.
     I do little and the company profits."

FIFTY-EIGHT

When people are led,
People are true.
When people are pushed or pulled,
They resist.

Therefore, the wise leader leads people
without pushing.
Moves others
without pulling.
Persuasive but not dominating;
Engaged but not ruthless.

FIFTY-NINE

When leading people
Remember your larger purpose.
The wise leader uses restraint
In mentoring others.
Helping others
Just enough.
Leading People
Just enough.
Never too much, never
too little.
Discover the Way in-between.

SIXTY

Leading an organization
Is like microwaving popcorn.
Attend to what you are doing
And nothing will burn.

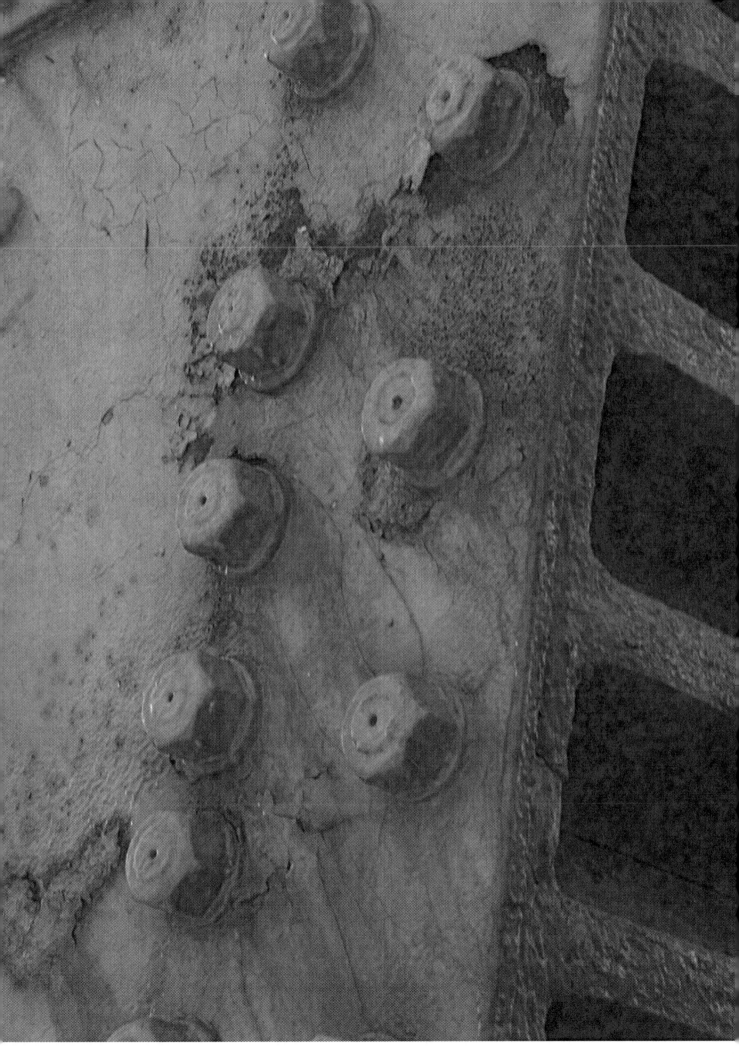

SIXTY-TWO

The wise leader remembers
The world around her.
You come from the All,
And return to the All.
A leader's purpose is to serve.

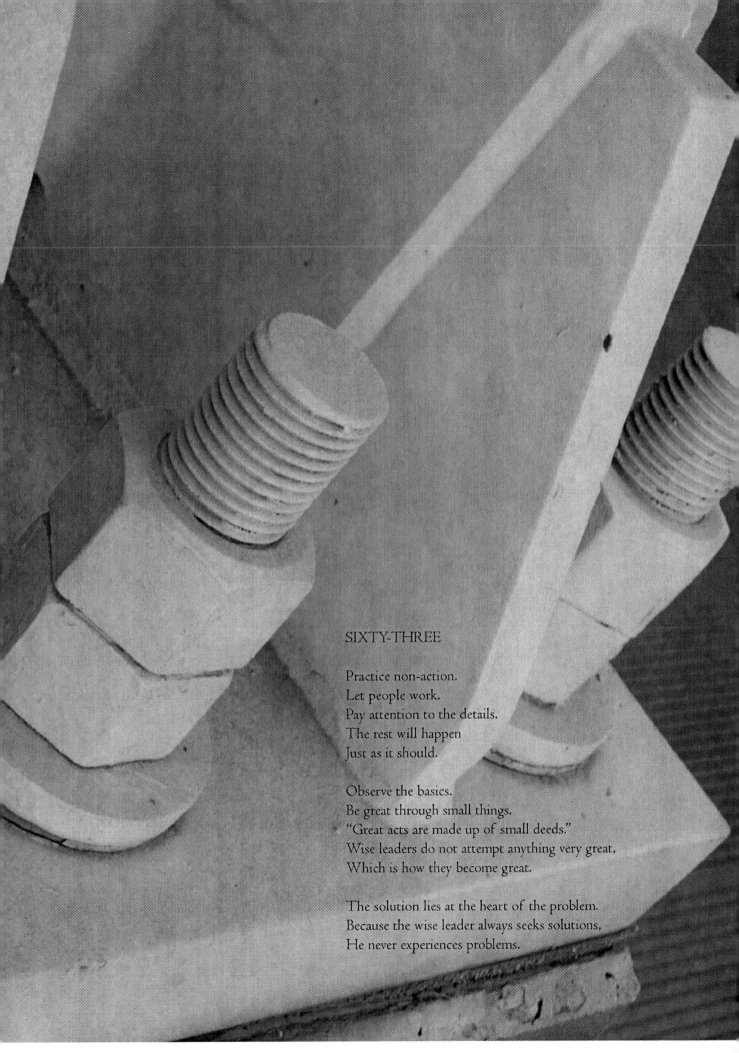

SIXTY-THREE

Practice non-action.
Let people work.
Pay attention to the details.
The rest will happen
Just as it should.

Observe the basics.
Be great through small things.
"Great acts are made up of small deeds."
Wise leaders do not attempt anything very great,
Which is how they become great.

The solution lies at the heart of the problem.
Because the wise leader always seeks solutions,
He never experiences problems.

SIXTY-FOUR

Smooth operations are easier to maintain.
Problems are simpler to prevent before they begin.
The hard is overcome;
Dilemmas dispersed.

Before confusion—
Before panic—
Manage the difficulty.

A multinational corporation begins with one person;
A billion dollar account starts with a single bill;
"A journey of a thousand miles starts under one's feet."

The leader who thinks will get in her own way;
If you do not blink, you cannot win.
The wise leader is not afraid to feel:
Great success.

Therefore, the wise leader holds her own opinion lightly.
She does not grasp ideas.
No winning, no losing.
She lets them go when they are done.

SIXTY-FIVE

A hundred years ago, leaders did not emotionally engage others
But simply paid them.
Why is leading people so hard these days?
Because people know.
Leaders who use force
Ruin the organization.
Those who lead without force
Discover success.
These are the two choices.
Leading People leads all back
Toward the One.

SIXTY-SIX

True leaders move beyond competing
And conquer everything.

Humility is the quality of the great leader.
To lead people, simply walk before them.
In this way, the people do not feel dragged;
They do not feel they are in danger.

When the true leader goes before people,
The people are safe.
Safe people succeed.

SIXTY-SEVEN

Some say the Way of Leading People is impossible.
I say, "Every leader counts."
With the newfound ability to destroy life on the Earth,
We no longer have the luxury of "impossible" as an excuse.

Three things I value:
Connection, flexibility, and respect.
When we lead with mutual recognition
And integrate our connection with others,
We reconcile the world to all beings, transcending time and space.

SIXTY-EIGHT

A strong leader never yells,
Never shames,
Never seeks revenge.
A great leader understands humility,
Not grandiose posturing or
Empty words.
This is what Leading People means.

SIXTY-NINE

A wise leader leads without
Appearing to lead—
Directs without using force.
Warriors of old understood this wisdom,
"To win without fighting is best."
By never fighting,
The great leader always wins.

SEVENTY

The Way of Leading People is not rocket science.
Yet few leaders actually know how.

Leaders who abuse others are praised.
Wealth built on the sweat of others is acclaimed.
How short-sighted!

"An eye for an eye makes the whole world blind."
This is the essence of Leading People.

SEVENTY-ONE

Paradox lies at the heart of Leading People.
Both "this" and "that."
Neither "this" nor "that."
True leaders discover the Middle Way.

SEVENTY-TWO

When people are not engaged,
The organization suffers.

Do not annoy people on the job.
Let them do what they were hired to do,
And they will consider you great.

A wise leader knows himself,
Trusts himself,
Neither boasting nor bragging.

SEVENTY-THREE

Why do some things work
While others fail?
This is simply the way of things.
Even the brightest leader does not always know.

SEVENTY-FOUR

If people hate their jobs,
Despise their leaders,
Attempting to intimidate them
Does little good.

SEVENTY-SIX

A newborn is gentle and flexible.
A corpse is hard and stiff.

Rigid and unyielding leaders bring death and loss to organizations,
While adaptable and flexible leaders brings profits and life.

A rigid organization cannot adapt.
Someone else enjoys their lunch.

Harsh and violent loses.
Flexible and yielding wins.

SEVENTY-SEVEN

Life gives breath without cost.
Greed charges for everything.

A great leader does not seek fame.
If distinction comes, then distinction comes.
She completes her work,
Sharing praise and wealth.

SEVENTY-EIGHT

Wise leaders learn from water.
Soothing and refreshing—
What is more common?
Ferociously cleansing—
What is more powerful?
Leading People is a mystery.

SEVENTY-NINE

When strong emotions arise, some aftermath is natural.
The great leader still knows his path.
Walking his path,
The difficult and arduous become clear.
He does not stray from the path.
This is what makes him a great leader.

EIGHTY

A leader leads
Then retires.
Another takes his place.
She will retire soon, too.
This is the Way of Leading People.

EIGHTY-ONE

Great leaders know they do not know.
Leaders who know are not great.
Serving others creates wealth.
Leading people brings riches.

About the Authors

Patrick and Timothy Warneka have been fascinated by the Asian martial arts from the moment they began hitting each other with sticks when they were little. (Things have pretty much gone downhill from there!) The brothers Warneka are founders of The Black Belt Consulting Group (BBCG), a leadership coaching, keynote speaking and consulting firm. BBCG helps people unlock their integral leadership skills through an exclusive combination the strength of Emotional Intelligence and the power of the philosophy embodied in the Asian martial arts.

A professional photographer living in Chicago for the last 18 years, PATRICK holds a black belt in Tae Kwon Do. Patrick has extensive experience in sales and customer service and has served as the President of the Chicago Hotel Concierge Association. Currently working at KPMG, in the past few years Patrick's architecture, stock, and portrait photography career has taken off to new heights. This is Patrick's first book.

TIMOTHY lives in Cleveland, Ohio with his wife and two children. Regarded as an expert in human performance, Tim is the author of the internationally-acclaimed *Leading People the Black Belt Way: Conquering the Five Core Problems Facing Leaders Today* and *Healing Katrina: Volunteering in Post-Hurricane Mississippi*. He has practiced Aikido since 1989 and holds black belt ranking. He has a bachelor's degree in psychology, a master's degree in counseling, certification as a massage professional, and post-graduate Gestalt certification. Tim is a visiting staff member at the Gestalt Institute of Cleveland and provides coaching, keynote speaking, and training around the U.S. His next goal is to provide these services on a global scale.

For more about The Black Belt Consulting Group
visit us: http://www.blackbeltconsultants.com

To discover success with Tim's other books, visit:
http://www.asogomi.com

A Note from the Authors

If you are interested in creating more success in your life and work using the principles of *The Way of Leading People*, you should strongly consider being coached by Tim. Tim coaches select leaders who are ready for greater success at work and in life. Tim's expert coaching takes place face-to-face, by phone, or by email. If you are selected to work with Tim, he'll create a customized approach specifically designed to meet your leadership goals and timeframes.

If you lead a book club, writers group, meditation group, photography club, Integral study group, martial arts club, or other similar group, we are happy to make ourselves available for an informative presentation and/or Q & A session ... often at no cost to your group. Tim is available in-person in Northeast Ohio, while Patrick is available in the Greater Chicagoland area. We are also quite willing to make ourselves available by phone or email to groups outside of these geographic areas.

Finally, if you would like to apply the post-rational principles contained in *The Way of Leading People* to your organization, we offer dynamic keynote speaking and strategic consulting processes designed to take your organization to the next level.

To learn more about any of these opportunities for creating success through the power of post-rational intelligence, feel free to contact us by phone at: (440) 944-4746, or email either of us personally at:

Tim's Email: timwarneka@yahoo.com
Patrick's Email: pjwarneka@yahoo.com.

We'll look forward to hearing from you!

Sincerely,

Patrick J. Warneka
Timothy H. Warneka

To learn more about Patrick's photography, visit him at:
http://www.patrickphotography.com

To learn more about how you can discover success by working
with Tim, visit him at:
http://www.timwarneka.com

Also by Tim Warneka...

Printed in the United States
78132LV00002B/251-324